SAILMAKER

SAILMAKER

by
Alan Spence

Hodder & Stoughton
A MEMBER OF THE HODDER HEADLINE GROUP

Performance Rights

Orders: please contact Bookpoint Ltd, 39 Milton Park, Abingdon, Oxon OX14 4TD. Telephone: (44) 01235 400414, Fax: (44) 01235 400454. Lines are open from 9.00-6.00, Monday to Saturday, with a 24 hour message answering service. Email address: orders@bookpoint.co.uk

British Library Cataloguing in Publication Data
A catalogue record for this title is available from The British Library

ISBN 0 340 49999 0

This edition first published 1998
Impression number   19 18 17 16 15 14 13
Year   2004 2003 2002 2001 2000

Typeset by Gecko Ltd, Bicester, Oxon.
Printed in Great Britain for Hodder & Stoughton Educational,
a division of Hodder Headline Plc, 338 Euston Road, London NW1 3BH
by Athenæum Press Ltd, Gateshead, Tyne & Wear.

SAILMAKER

Scene

The setting of the play alternates between a Glasgow tenement flat (room and kitchen) and its surrounding streets and back courts.

The play begins in the early 1960s and continues through that decade.

Cast

DAVIE

A middle-aged Glasgow man, a former sailmaker

ALEC

Davie's son

IAN

Alec's cousin

BILLY

Ian's father, Davie's younger brother

This play was first performed at the Traverse Theatre Club, Edinburgh, on 29 April 1982.

Act one

Dark. Light on ALEC, centre stage.

ALEC   Sometimes I wake up in the middle of the night and I can remember it. The feeling.
        I was only a boy. Eleven.
        There was this knock at the door. The middle of the night. Batter. Batter.
        It was a policeman. He said my mother had taken a turn for the worse. My father had to go down to the hospital.
        I couldn't get back to sleep.
        It was getting light by the time he came back . . .

(Lights fade up. DAVIE enters, stands behind ALEC)

DAVIE   Ah've got a bit of bad news for ye son. Yer mammy's dead.

ALEC   Part of me already knew, accepted it. Part of me couldn't. Part of me cried.

DAVIE   Ah've got a bit of bad news for ye son.

ALEC   I cried and a numbness came on me, shielding me from the real pain.

DAVIE   Yer mammy's dead.

ALEC   I was standing there, crying – real big deep sobs. But the other part of me, the part that accepted, was just watching.

DAVIE   Ah've got a bit of bad news for ye son.

ALEC   I was watching myself crying, watching my puny grief from somewhere above it all. I was me and I was not-me.

DAVIE   Yer mammy's dead.

              (ALEC turns to face him)

              There's just you an me now son. We'll have tae make the best of it. *(Turns away)*

              Ah'll make some breakfast.

ALEC   Ah'm no really very hungry.

DAVIE   Naw. Ah'll make a cuppa tea.

              (Moves back, quietly busies himself, sets fire in hearth)

ALEC   Later on I opened the window and looked out across the back courts. The breeze was warm. Everything was the same. It was very ordinary. Nothing had changed. I don't know what I had expected. A sign. Jesus to come walking across the back and tell me everything was all right. A window in the sky to open and God to lean out and say my mother had arrived safe. The sun shone on the grey tenements, on the railings and the middens, on the dustbins and the spilled ashes. It glinted on windows and on bits of broken glass. It was like something I remembered, something from a dream. Across the back, a wee boy was standing, blowing on a mouth-organ, playing the same two notes over and over again.

(Two notes on mouth-organ, repeated, continuing while he talks)

> My mother was dead.
> My mother was dead.
> The breeze touched my cheek. It scattered the ashes round the midden. It ruffled the clothes of the wee boy standing there, playing his two notes.
> Over and over and over.
> I looked up at the sky, the clouds moving across. Just for a minute a gap opened up, a wee patch of clear blue.

(Two notes continuing, then fade)

DAVIE   We better get this place tidied up a bit son. Folk'll be comin back after the funeral.

(Moves around as he is talking – ALEC remains static)

As long as ye keep movin it doesnae hit ye. Get the fire goin clean the windaes dust the furniture think about somethin for eating don't stop keep yerself goin. Sometimes for whole minutes ye can nearly nearly forget about it, shove it tae the back ae yer mind. Then maybe yer lookin for somethin and ye turn round tae ask her where it is an ye wonder for a minute where she's got tae and ye think maybe she's through in the room an ye catch yerself thinkin it and it hits ye an ye think Christ this is it this is me for the rest ae ma days.

ALEC   After the funeral. Back hame. House full ae people. Aunties an Uncles. Folk we hadnae seen for years. On and on and on.

DAVIE   That's it. They're aw away. Just you an me now son.

ALEC   Aye.

DAVIE   God, Ah'm shattered.
Isn't it funny the words ye use tae describe things. Shattered! *(Looking round.)* Place is in a right mess, eh? Still. Never mind. We can clear it up in the mornin, eh? Ach aye.
In the mornin. *(Exit)*

(Lights up. IAN enters, running)

ALEC   Ah had a yacht. Y'ought tae see it. *(Runs out for yacht)*

IAN   Put it in the canal. Ye can all see it.

ALEC   *(Comes back with yacht)* There!

IAN   Is that it?

ALEC   Aye. Ah found it in the Glory Hole.

IAN   *(Takes yacht, examines it)* It's got nae sails or nae mast or nothin.

ALEC   *(Takes yacht back)* Ah'm gonnae get ma da tae fix it up. Ma da's a sailmaker.

IAN   Your da sells stuff on the never never and collects the money roon the doors. He's a tick man.

ALEC   He's workin as a tick man. But he's really a sailmaker. That's his *real* job. That's his trade.

IAN	How come he disnae work at it?
ALEC	Don't know. Maybe there's nae jobs.
IAN	Ye need a trade. That's what ma da says. He's gonnae get me in wi him at the paintin when ah'm auld enough.
ALEC	Maybe ma da'll go back tae his trade. (*Holds up yacht*) That was a great poem he made up.
IAN	Your da?
ALEC	(*Nods*) Ah had a yacht Y'ought tae see it
IAN	Your da didnae write that!
ALEC	Aye he did!
IAN	He didnae!
ALEC	He did!
IAN	Well how come ah've heard it?
ALEC	Maybe ma da told your da.
IAN	Aye, Maybe! (*Sarcastic*)
ALEC	Ye know, they must have had sailmakers away way way back in the aulden days, when there wis pirates an explorers an that. Right back . . .
IAN	Roman Galleys . . .
ALEC	Vikings!
IAN	When's yer da gonnae fix it up?
ALEC	Soon.
IAN	Ah can just see it. It would look great wi red sails. Just like the song.
ALEC	Eh?
IAN	There's a record. Red sails in the sunset.
ALEC	That's right, ah've heard it.
IAN	It's great. (*Sings*) Red sails in the sunset.
ALEC	(*Joining in*) Way out on the sea (*waves boat up and down in time. They laugh, self-conscious. ALEC brings boat down to rest on floor, face down.*)
ALEC	Used to be Jacky's. Ah got it when he went tae America.
IAN	Aw his stuff got shared oot. Ah got his soldiers.
ALEC	Did ye?
IAN	He's ma cousin tae, ye know. You're no the only wan!
ALEC	Must be great in America, eh?
IAN	Cowboys and gangsters an that.
ALEC	Magic.

IAN	Hey look, it's a submarine. (*Pushes yacht forward*) German battleship on the port bow. Prepare to torpedo.
ALEC	They're firing depth charges! Dive! Dive! Dive!
	(*IAN makes explosion noises, 'blows up' yacht*)
ALEC	(*Taking yacht again*)It's a shark. It's gonnae get ye! (*Attacks IAN with it, going for his throat*)
IAN	Aaaaaargh! (*They lose interest in the game*)
	Hey, have you got any new comics tae swop?
ALEC	Ah got some in a parcel fae Jacky, but ah don't want tae swop them.
IAN	How no?
ALEC	They're real American wans. They're coloured. Ah don't want tae swop them for scabby auld black and white things.
IAN	But Jacky sent me some tae. We could just dae a straight swop.
ALEC	What've ye got?
IAN	Superman. Blackhawk.
ALEC	Ah've got some Superman as well. An a coupla Batman. An a Creepy Worlds.
IAN	Yer on!
ALEC	After tea?
IAN	Right! (*They spit on their palms and shake hands, clinching the deal*)
ALEC	Ma da's quite late. Maybe he's gettin fish suppers for the tea.
IAN	Fish suppers? In the middle of the week?
ALEC	He's no very good at cookin.
IAN	Oh aye.
ALEC	Hey! Ah've got some great new foties for ma Rangers scrapbook. (*Shows IAN book*)
IAN	Where d'ye get the big coloured wan ae the team?
ALEC	In the Rangers handbook. It's a beauty, eh?
IAN	Brilliant.
ALEC	Blue really is the best colour.
IAN	That's what ma da says. He says it's God's favourite colour! Cause the sky's blue, and that's where God lives.
ALEC	Sea's blue as well. Look, ye even get blue in the fire – see thae blue flames there! Pity the grass is green.
IAN	But ye can get blue grass.
ALEC	Can ye?

IAN	They've got it in America. There's a group called Johnny Duncan and the Bluegrass Boys. They dae sorta country and western.

ALEC	That's right. (Sings)
	    Last train to San Fernando
	    Last train to San Fernando

IAN	(Joins in)
	    If you miss this one
	    You'll never get another one
	    Beedi Beedi Bum Bum
	    To San Fernando

ALEC	Hey, they should get some ae that blue grass for Ibrox!
IAN	Can ye imagine it!
ALEC	Ah've got somethin else ah wanted tae show ye. It's blue as well.
IAN	(Looks at what ALEC has in his hand and recoils) It's a holy medal!
ALEC	Our Lady.
IAN	Whit ye daein wi that?
ALEC	Ah found it.
IAN	Whit did ye keep it for?
ALEC	A just sorta . . . liked it.
IAN	Ye should fling it away. It'll bring ye bad luck.
ALEC	The middle part's blue . . . see. That's the colour ae Mary, the mother ae God.
IAN	How d'ye know that?
ALEC	Maureen told me.
IAN	(Knowing) Oh aye! So that's it, eh?
ALEC	What?
IAN	Ye've got a fancy for wee Maureen!
ALEC	Ah just . . . like her.
IAN	Next thing ye'll be carryin a rosary and crossin yerself!
ALEC	Don't be stupid! (IAN laughs, ALEC shuts scrapbook, turns away)
IAN	Hey c'mon! Don't take the huff! (Coaxing) Hey, what are we gonnae sing at the Lifeboys concert?
ALEC	Don't know.
IAN	How about that wan we were singin? Last train to San Fernando.
ALEC	Don't really know it. Just the chorus.
IAN	Me tae. How about Singing the Blues? Ye must know that.
ALEC	Aye.
IAN	An blue's yer favourite colour, right?

ALEC	Aye. Funny how blue means sad, intit. It's no really a sad song but.
IAN	(*Sings*) Ah never felt more like singin the blues Cos I never thought that I'd ever lose Your love babe You got me singing the blues
ALEC	Ah never felt more like cryin all night Cos everythin's wrong an nothin is right Without you You got me singin the blues (*Sing together*) The moon and stars no longer shine The dream is gone I thought was mine There's nothin left for me to do But cry-y-y-y over you
ALEC	Ah'll tell ye somethin. It's a secret but. Don't tell anybody.
IAN	Awright.
ALEC	Promise?
IAN	Cross ma heart.
ALEC	It was after ma mammy died. Ah was lookin at the sky above oor hoose. An ah thought ah saw her.
IAN	Yer Ma?
ALEC	Mary. Our Lady. Dressed aw in blue, Ah couldnae be sure. But ah thought it was.
IAN	Above your hoose?
ALEC	Just for a second.
IAN	That's creepy. Did ye have that medal wi ye?
ALEC	Aye.
IAN	Maybe that's what did it. Put the idea intae yer heid.
ALEC	Maybe.
IAN	Ma da says when he dies he's gonnae get his ashes scattered on the pitch at Ibrox. (*Both half-smile*)
ALEC	Show ye somethin else. (*Goes to glory hole, comes back with canvas bag, holds up shell*) This used tae be ma mammy's.
IAN	Some size eh. (*Takes shell*) Imagine the size ae the whelk ye'd get out ae that!
ALEC	Ah hate whelks. (*IAN mimics picking out giant whelk, wriggling it, eating it. ALEC snatches shell back*)

	If ye listen ye can hear the sea. (*Holds shell to his ear, then passes it back to* IAN)
IAN	(*Holding shell to ear*) So ye can. Wonder what sea it is?
ALEC	The Pacific. Naw, the Indian Ocean. (*Holds up shell*) Amazin colours. It's like . . . when the light shines on a patch ae oil on the street.
	(*Takes out sheet of cellophane*) See this?
IAN	Cellophane.
ALEC	My ma used tae bring it hame when she worked in the bakery. Sheets an sheets ae it. They used it for wrappin cakes. Look . . . What colour is it?
IAN	Gold.
ALEC	Right. Watch! (*Opens it out*) Da raaa! See! It's clear. See right through it. Fold it up tight. (*Folds*) An it's gold again.
IAN	Aye right enough. Ah've noticed that.
ALEC	Wonder how it works. Where the colour goes.
ALEC	Did ah ever show ye ma da's sailmakin tools?
IAN	Naw, (*Shows* IAN *tools*)
	These are called marlinspikes. Great name, eh?
IAN	(*Takes marlinspike, weighs it in his hand*)
	Make a great chib!
ALEC	(*Takes another marlinspike from bag*)
	Fence ye
	(*They cross swords, fence with much clashing of blades*)
	Swine!
IAN	Dog!
ALEC	Scurvy knave! Ah'll have ye keel-hauled!
IAN	Fifty lashes!
ALEC	Clap ye in irons!
IAN	Make ye walk the plank!
	(*They continue fencing,* DAVIE *enters*)
DAVIE	Boys! Boys! Ye'll poke each other's eyes oot!
	(*Last clash of blades, then they stop*)
	Right. That's better. (*Looks at tools*) Where did ye get these anyway?
ALEC	In the Glory Hole.
IAN	Ah better be goin in for ma tea.
ALEC	Don't forget the comics.

| | (*Sees* IAN *out*) |

DAVIE (*Picks up tools*)

Marlinspikes.

ALEC (*Coming over*)

You've been drinkin. Ah can smell it.

DAVIE (*Breathes at him*) Just wan, son. Honest! Wee half at the end ae the day. Just helps me tae unwind. Up an doon stairs aw day, knockin folk's doors. Half ae them hide when they hear ye comin. Shove the light aff, shoosh the weans. (*Whispers*) Sssshhh! It's the tick man! Ah don't know.
(*Holds wooden fid in hand*) This is a fid. Made fae lignum vitae. Hardest wood in the world. Used it for splicin rope.

ALEC What's this! (*Holds up leather palm*)

DAVIE It's a palm. For shovin needles through the canvas.

ALEC Ah was kiddin on it was a sorta glove. For fightin.

DAVIE (*Laughs*) Knuckleduster!

ALEC How come ye chucked yer trade?

DAVIE It chucked me! The chandlers ah worked for shut doon. Ah got laid off. That was it. Nothin else doin. Nae work. Naebody needs sailmakers these days.

ALEC (*Holds up yacht*) Could ye make me a sail for this? Ah found it in the Glory Hole tae. Ah thought you could fix it up.

DAVIE Oh aye. It's a beauty, eh? Be nice, aw rigged out.
Can sail it in the park.
Course, it'll take time. Materials'll be dear. But ah'll see what ah can do.

ALEC When?

DAVIE Wait an see. (*Hands back yacht*) Who knows? Maybe ma coupon'll come up this week!

ALEC Remember the last time ye won?

DAVIE First dividend. Two quid!
Ah didnae let it go tae ma head mind! Didnae chuck ma job. Didnae buy a villa in the south of France. Ah think every second game was a draw that week! Never mind. Some ae these days.

(*DAVIE sits down, takes newspaper and scrap of paper from his briefcase, writes*)

Ah didnae bring in anythin for the tea. D'ye fancy nippin doon tae the chippy, gettin a coupla fish suppers?

ALEC Awright.

(*DAVIE hands him money*)

Can ah get a pickle?

DAVIE Get anythin ye like. Here's somethin else ye can do for me.

	Themorra at dinnertime. Take this line tae the bookie.
ALEC	Och da!
DAVIE	Whit's the matter?
ALEC	It's just that . . . ah don't *like* that bookie. He's creepy.
DAVIE	Away ye go!
ALEC	An that back close where he has his pitch is aw horrible an smelly.
DAVIE	(*Waves his line*) But this could be worth a fortune! Three doubles, a treble, an accumulator. If it comes up we're laughin. Here son, ah'll leave it here wi the money inside it.
ALEC	(*Picks up line, reads it*) Why d'ye always write Mainsail at the bottom ae yer line?
DAVIE	That's what ye call a nom-de-plume. The bettin's illegal ye see. The bookie gets done fae time tae time. An if you put yer real name on the line, the polis might book you as well. So ye use a made-up name.
ALEC	Mainsail
	(*Pockets line*)
	(ALEC *comes forward,* IAN *enters with football which he passes to* ALEC)
IAN	A wee game!
ALEC	Heidy fitba!
IAN	Right, ah'm Rangers. You can be Celtic.
ALEC	You're always Rangers!
IAN	It's ma baw isn't it.
ALEC	Ah'm no goin Celtic. Ah'll be . . . Real Madrid.
IAN	Suit yerself. Ah'll still beat ye!
	(*They play, heading and kicking the ball back and forth*)
ALEC	Aw shite! Ah just remembered.
IAN	Whit!
ALEC	Ah'm supposed tae take ma da's line doon tae the bookie. Comin wi me?
IAN	Aye, awright.
	(*They walk*)
ALEC	Ah hate gawn.
IAN	How?
ALEC	Don't know. Ah just don't like the bookie. See when ah was dead wee, ah used to hear ma da talkin aboot the bookie, only ah didnae know what it meant, an ah thought he wis saying boogie.
IAN	Like the boogies ye pick oot yer nose?

ALEC	Aye!
	(*They laugh*)
IAN	Whit did ye think he wis, a wee guy covered in snotters?!
	(*Wails, waves his hands towards* ALEC)
	The boogie man's gonnae get ye!
ALEC	That's the thing tae. They were always tellin me tae watch out or the bogie man would get me. An ah must've got the two things mixed up.
IAN	Daftie!
ALEC	Tell ye somethin else ah thought as well. When ma da used tae talk aboot tryin the pools, ah always imagined him fishin in these big deep pools a watter.
IAN	Fishin!
ALEC	Aye.
IAN	Whit a diddy!
ALEC	Ah'm talkin aboot when ah wis wee!
IAN	(*Laughs*) Bogeymen an pools a watter!
ALEC	Cannae tell you anythin!
	(*Turns away*)
IAN	C'mon, ah'll race ye!
	(*They turn, skid to a halt*)
	Is this the close?
ALEC	Ye can tell by the smell!
	Make sure ah've got the line.
IAN	The fishin line!
	(ALEC *swipes at him, he dodges back*)
	Watch out for the bogie man! He'll shove ye in the pool!
	(ALEC *chases him offstage*)
	(*Enter* DAVIE *and* BILLY, *talking as they walk*)
DAVIE	Eh, Billy . . . that coupla quid ah tapped off ye. Could it wait till next week?
BILLY	Aye sure.
DAVIE	Things are still a wee bit tight.
BILLY	What's the score?
DAVIE	Eh?
BILLY	Ye shouldnae be this skint. What is it?
DAVIE	Ah told ye. It's the job. Just hasnae been so great. No sellin enough. No collectin enough. No gettin much over the basic.

BILLY	Aye, but ye should be able tae get by. Just the two ae ye.
DAVIE	It's no easy.
BILLY	Ye bevvyin?
DAVIE	Just a wee half when ah finish ma work. An by Christ ah need it.
BILLY	Ye bettin too heavy? Is that it?
DAVIE	(*Hesitates then decides to tell him*) It started a coupla months ago. Backed a favourite. Absolute surefire certainty. Couldnae lose. But it was even money, so ah had tae put quite a whack on it. (*Slightly shamefaced*) Best part ae a week's wages.
BILLY	An it got beat?
DAVIE	Out the park. So ah made it up by borrowin off the bookie. He does his moneylender on the side. Charges interest.
BILLY	An every week ye miss the interest goes up.
DAVIE	This is it. Now when ah pay him ah'm just clearin the interest. Ah'm no even touchin the original amount ah borrowed. Ah must've paid him back two or three times over, an ah still owe him the full whack.
BILLY	Bastard, eh? Sicken ye. *And* he's a pape.
	(DAVIE *laughs*)
DAVIE	Still, Aw ah need's a wee turn. Ah mean ma luck's got tae change sometime hasn't it? Law of averages.
BILLY	Whatever that is.
DAVIE	Things have got tae get better.
BILLY	It's a mugs game. The punter canny win.
DAVIE	Got tae keep tryin.
BILLY	Flingin it away! Look, Don't get me wrong. Ah don't mind helpin ye out, but ah'm no exactly rollin in it maself.
DAVIE	You'll get yer money back.
BILLY	That's no what ah mean!
DAVIE	What am ah supposed tae dae? Get a job as a company director or somethin! Ah'll go doon tae the broo in the mornin!
BILLY	There must be some way tae get this bookie aff yer back for a start.
DAVIE	Aye sure!
BILLY	Ah mean, you've paid him.
DAVIE	Ah knew his terms.
BILLY	It's no even legal.
DAVIE	Neither is gettin his heavies tae kick folk's heids in.
BILLY	So maybe he's no the only wan that knows a few hard men.

DAVIE	(*Sighs*) What a carry on, eh?
BILLY	Hey. Remember when we were wee, we used to fight like cat an dog?
DAVIE	Ah could beat ye an all!
BILLY	Oh aye, ye were too fast for me. Quick on yer feet. The old one-two. Ma only chance was tae get ye in a bearhug.
DAVIE	Ah've still got the bruises!
BILLY	Ah remember one time we were havin a right old barney, an da was tryin tae sleep – must've been on the nightshift. An he came runnin out the room in his shirt-tail an clattered the pair ae us!
DAVIE	He was a tough auld customer right enough. Had tae be in these days.
BILLY	D'ye know he *walked* fae Campbeltown tae Glasgow tae get a start in the yards! Tellin ye, we don't know we're livin. Ah hear the boy's daein well at school.
DAVIE	Oh aye. He's clever. He'll get on.
BILLY	He'll get on a lot better if you screw the heid, right?
DAVIE	C'mon Billy, ah dae ma best. It's just . . .
BILLY	Ah know it's hard on yer own an that . . .
DAVIE	Naw ye don't know. Naebody knows, unless they've been through it. (*Quieter*) Comin hame's the worst. The boy's oot playin. Hoose is empty. Gets on top of ye. The other night there, ah got this queer feelin. Ah felt as if aw the furniture and everythin was *watching* me. Sounds daft, eh? Maybe ah'm goin aff ma heid!
BILLY	Bound tae take a while tae get over it.
DAVIE	If ah ever dae.
	(*They cross to where ALEC is playing with yacht*)
BILLY	(*To ALEC*) How ye doin wee yin? What's this ye've got? (*Picks up yacht*)
ALEC	Used tae be Jacky's.
DAVIE	Ah'm gonnae fix it up, when ah've got the time.
ALEC	Ye've been sayin that for weeks!
BILLY	Ah could paint it if ye like.
ALEC	Would ye?
BILLY	Aye, sure. Should come up really nice. Ah'll take it away wi me. Get it done this week.
ALEC	This week!
BILLY	Nae bother.
ALEC	What colours will ye make it?

BILLY	Ah think the hull has tae be white. Ah've got a nice white gloss at work. The keel ah could dae in blue. Maybe put a wee blue rim round the edge here. An ah think ah've got a light brown that would do just fine for the deck. That suit ye awright?
ALEC	Great!
BILLY	Ye won't even recognise it. It'll be like a brand new boat.
ALEC	It'll be dead real, eh?
BILLY	It'll be that real we can aw sail away in it!
DAVIE	Away tae Never Never Land!
BILLY	Right, ah'll be seein ye.
	(*Takes yacht, exits*)
	(ALEC *follows him seeing him out, then comes back*)
ALEC	Uncle Billy's great isn't he.
DAVIE	Ach aye. Mind you, he's pure mental when it comes tae Rangers an aw that. Big Orange headbanger. But yer right. Underneath it he's a good lad. Solid.
	(ALEC *gets ready to go, puts leather palm on hand, tucks marlinspike under his belt*)
	Where ye goin?
ALEC	Out tae play wi Ian. See you later.
	(*Comes forward,* IAN *enters carrying four lengths of bamboo cane*)
IAN	Ah've got the string an the bits ae cane.
ALEC	Great! Have ye got the hacksaw blade?
IAN	Aye. Have you got the tape?
ALEC	Aye.
IAN	Right. You make the bows an ah'll make the arras. D'ye know how tae dae it?
ALEC	Aye.
IAN	Ye pit a wee notch at baith ends, for the string. Then ye wind a wee bit tape roon, so the cane disnae split . . .
ALEC	Ah know! (*Sets to work, notches ends*)
IAN	Hurry up wi the blade. Ah need it.
ALEC	Whit fur?
IAN	Ye've got tae cut through the cane. If ye just break it in two, it aw splits, just makes a mess. (*Takes blade and saws*)
ALEC	Terrible noise it makes.
IAN	Sets yer teeth on edge.
ALEC	Like polystyrene when ye rub it on the windae. Like the teacher's chalk when it scrapes on the blackboard . . .

IAN	Don't talk aboot school. Ah hate it! Hey, comin we'll no bother goin back on Monday? We'll just run away and dog it forever!
ALEC	That would be brilliant! Where could we go?
IAN	We could go tae America and live wi *real* Indians. Jacky would help us.
ALEC	Ach, there's nae real Indians left. They aw get pit oot in daft wee reservations.
IAN	How aboot India then? Or Africa? We could live in a tree hoose.
ALEC	Pick bananas an oranges.
IAN	Hunt animals.
ALEC	Make pals wi some ae them but. Lions an tigers an that.
IAN	Make pals wi the darkies tae.
ALEC	Great white chiefs.
IAN	(*Beating chest*) Me chief Ian!
ALEC	We'd have tae gie wursels better names but.
IAN	Walla Walla Wooski!
ALEC	We could paint wursels tae. Wear feathers an bones.
IAN	Imagine bein cannibals. We could just eat white men that got lost in the jungle.
ALEC	Fancy goin intae the chippy an askin for two single fish an a whiteman supper!
IAN	Sausage rolls wi pricks in them!
ALEC	That's horrible!
IAN	Imagine fat Louie cuttin people up for pies!
ALEC	Like Sweeney Todd.
IAN	People are supposed tae taste like pork.
ALEC	Think ah'll stop eatin meat.
IAN	Ach don't be daft!
	(*While talking, they have been carrying on with their work*)
ALEC	(*Flexing bow*) There!
IAN	(*Holds up arrows*) Right!
	(*ALEC passes bow to IAN, who fires arrow*)
IAN	It's a goodyin.
ALEC	Gie me a shot.
	(*Takes bow, fires low shot*)
	C'mon we'll go huntin!
	(*They exit*)

(DAVIE in chair. BILLY enters, carrying yacht in bag)

BILLY	Hey Davie, ah brought ye a coupla cowboy books. Ah know ye go in for the highbrow stuff. Dickens an that. But these are a good read.
DAVIE	Och naw. Ah'll read anything. Shane. That's a goodyin. Saw the picture.
BILLY	Alan Ladd, eh? Great stuff. Terrific.

(Enter ALEC)

There yar then! (*Holds out yacht*)

ALEC	Look at that! It's just like new.
BILLY	What did ah tell ye?
DAVIE	Ye did a nice job Billy. It's beaufiful.
ALEC	Brilliant. (*Holds yacht, amazed*)
BILLY	Blue an white. Best colours in the world.
ALEC	Blue's ma favourite colour.
BILLY	There yar! The boy's got sense!
ALEC	Orange is good as well, isn't it?
BILLY	Orange is *great*!
ALEC	How about purple?
BILLY	Oh aye, purple's good.
ALEC	Red?
BILLY	Red's fine. So's yellow.
ALEC	Black an white?
BILLY	They're OK. They're no exactly good an they're no exactly bad. They're sorta . . . nothingy. But there's one colour we havenae mentioned, an that's the worst ae the lot, an that's . . . green! Ye don't like green do ye?
ALEC	No really.
BILLY	Terrible colour.
DAVIE	Away ye go! How can a colour be bad? Just because Catholics wear it.
BILLY	It's maybe no bad in itself, but they Catholics have made it bad.
DAVIE	Even Rangers play on green grass!
BILLY	Aye, they trample it under their feet!
DAVIE	It takes a green stem tae haud up an orange lily!
BILLY	Aye, well. The exception proves the rule, doesn't it!
DAVIE	(*Tuts*) Ach! Fillin the boy's head wi rubbish.
BILLY	(*To ALEC*) Anyway, there's yer yacht. An blue and white it is!

ALEC	(*To* DAVIE) Now will ye fix it up?
DAVIE	Be a shame not to. (*Crouches down*) Need to bring the mainmast up about here. Drill a wee hole in the deck, fit it in. Fix on a bowsprit for the jib, bring out a boom for the mainsail. Can work out the length an get dowelling cut to size. Taper it. Then there's the riggin, an material for the sails . . .
ALEC	Red!
BILLY	That'll make it red white and blue. Great!
DAVIE	Ye'll have tae give it a name.
BILLY	How about *No Surrender*
DAVIE	Sometimes they're called after the places they're built. *City of Glasgow.*
ALEC	Ah thought ae a name. *Star of the Sea.*
DAVIE	That's nice.
BILLY	Did ye make it up?
ALEC	Ah read it in a book.
BILLY	Oh aye. Its no bad right enough. But ah still prefer *No Surrender.*
DAVIE	Aye, you would!
	(ALEC *makes boat sail*)
BILLY	Eh . . . (*To* DAVIE) ah had a word wi that bookie, about the wee . . . business.
DAVIE	What did he say?
BILLY	Och, he tried tae come the hard man. But ah don't think he'll bother ye again.
DAVIE	Thanks.
BILLY	See ye. (*To* ALEC) Cheerio wee yin.
ALEC	Cheerio. An thanks.
BILLY	Nae bother.
	(*Exit*)
ALEC	(*To* DAVIE) When ye gonnae fix it?
DAVIE	(*Cheerful*) Soon. Just you wait an see!
	(*Dark. Light on* DAVIE, *forward*)
DAVIE	It was wan a thae dark closes. Nae lights workin. Stink fae the back close – drains an cats an God knows what. That's where they were waitin. Heard a noise an they were comin at me. Two ae them. In wi the heid, the boot. Slammed me against the wa. Butt in the face. They grabbed ma briefcase. Ah swung wi the torch, got one ae them. Ya Bastard. Brained him. Then they got me down. Kicked me in the ribs. Got off their marks an left me. Took ma briefcase. Tick money. The lot. Everything except ma torch.

(*Lights come up a little, ALEC takes torch*)

ALEC   It's got a dent in it.

DAVIE   Guy must have had a thick skull!

(*ALEC wields torch like club*)

Ah've seen the day when ah could've stiffened the pair ae them. Used tae be pretty useful. Flyweight. Ah knew Benny Lynch ye know. Tapped me for ten bob the week before he died.

(*ALEC is shining torch round about*)

Don't waste the batteries son.

(*ALEC switches off torch. Cut lights. Dark*)

(*ALEC, DAVIE, BILLY, IAN, home from the football match*)

BILLY   (*Sings*)
Sure it's old but it is beautiful
And its colours they are fine . . .

DAVIE   Christsake Billy, ye'll get us hung!

BILLY   It's a protestant country isn't it? An ah'm not ashamed tae show ma colours. (*more conversational tone*) Wasnae a bad game aw the same.

DAVIE   Well, it wasnae exactly the greatest Rangers team ah've seen.

BILLY   Now Willie Thornton, there was a centre forward. Wan game, they were playin Celtic at Ibrox. Nothin each, a minute tae go. Waddell gets it tae the byeline an slings it across, and there's Thornton comin in like a bullet. An'm no kiddin ye, he just dived full-length, met the baw aboot that height aff the grun. Just rocketed aff his heid an intae the net. Keeper never got a sniff at it. An there wis Thornton, face doon in the mud – must've been embedded in it, aboot six inches deep. They had tae prise him oot!
    That was some team they had then. Wee Torry Gillick at inside right. Waddell on the wing. An the defence! Big George Young, Sammy Cox, Tiger Shaw, big Woodburn before he got suspended. There were like . . . iron.

DAVIE   'They shall not pass!'

BILLY   An if the other team *did* get through, there was Jerry Dawson tae stop them. What a keeper!

DAVIE   Ah remember wance, he was aff his line, an the forward comin in just lobbed him – cheeky as ye like – just flicked it over his heid. It was goin, aw the way . . . Christ, does Jerry no fling himself *backwards* – ah'm no kiddin ye, right back like that, parallel tae the grun, and he clutched it, about an inch fae the line. Talk about acrobatic! Never seen anythin like it!

IAN   Did ye ever see Alan Morton?

DAVIE   The wee blue devil! Oh aye, ah saw him when ah was wee. He was one ae the Wembley Wizards. A real ballplayer, ye know what ah mean? Pure skill. An it wasnae so easy then – the baw was heavier an they aw wore these big clumpetty boots up tae here. But ye should've seen the wee man dribblin. Incredible! An wan time he scored direct fae a corner kick. Curved it right in. Magic!

ALEC   Charlie Tully did that.

DAVIE   Don't talk tae me about Tully! Morton was in a different class. He was a real gentleman tae. Never committed a deliberate foul in his life.

BILLY   A protestant!

(*They laugh. Boys take imaginary ball and run across stage. DAVIE and BILLY go out*)

ALEC   C'mon, ah'll be Alan Morton, you be Willie Thornton.

IAN   But they didnae play at the same time.

ALEC   Disnae matter. We can kid on. Use yer imagination.

IAN   Awright, it's the greatest Rangers team of all time, gathered together for one special game.

ALEC   The Championship of the Universe!

IAN   Playin on the moon.

ALEC   Against Martian Celtic! Biggest buncha zombies ye ever saw!

IAN   Everybody's weightless. Morton crosses an Thornton jumps 50 feet in the air.

ALEC   He misses and the baw goes into orbit.

IAN   So they bring on a new baw. Weighs half a ton

ALEC   They're aw wearin lead boots. There's been some terrible tackles.

IAN   The Martian goalie's got eight arms and six legs.

ALEC   The centre-forward's got four heids.

IAN   Typical fenians!

ALEC   We're intae injury time. Morton's got the ball. (*Dribbles*) He beats one tackle, beats two, passes it to Thornton. (*Passes*)

IAN   Back to Morton. (*Passes*)

ALEC   To Thornton. (*Passes*)

IAN   To Morton. (*Passes*)

ALEC   The goalie comes rushin out. He's about ten feet four. Morton slips it through his three pairs of legs, gives it back to Thornton. (*Passes*)

IAN   (*Shoots*) An it's a goal!

ALEC   An there goes the final whistle. It's all over. Rangers are the champions of the whole Universe!

IAN   Ea-sy!

ALEC	See! Ah told ye ye could use yer imagination.
IAN	Imagine *really* bein a fitba player. Gettin *paid* for it! Be better than anythin.
ALEC	Best job in the whole world.
IAN	Better than bein a painter!
ALEC	Or a sailmaker.
IAN	Or a tick man.
	(*They exit, DAVIE and BILLY enter, opposite sides of stage*)
BILLY	What's up wi your face?
	(DAVIE *shakes head*)
	What's the matter?
DAVIE	Ah just got ma jotters. Week's notice.
BILLY	Jesus Christ! What for?
DAVIE	Ach! They're sayin the book's a dead loss. They're gonnae shut it awthegether. Put the sheriff's officers on tae the folk that still owe money.
BILLY	Bastards.
DAVIE	Gettin that doin just finished it. Losin the money an the ledgers an everythin.
BILLY	But that wasnae your fault!
DAVIE	Try tellin them that! So that's me. Scrubbed. Again. Laid off. Redundant. Services no longer required. Just like that. Ah don't know. Work aw yer days an what've ye got tae show for it? Turn roon an kick ye in the teeth. Ah mean, what *have* ye got when ye come right down tae it. Nothin.
BILLY	Ah might be able tae get ye a start in our place. Cannae promise mind ye. An if there was anythin it wouldnae be much. Maybe doin yer sweeper up or that.
DAVIE	Anythin's better than nothin.
BILLY	An once yer in the place, ye never know. Somethin better might come up.
DAVIE	(*Dead*) Aye.
BILLY	Likes ae a storeman's job or that.
DAVIE	Aye.
BILLY	We never died a winter yet, eh?
	(DAVIE *nods*. BILLY *exits*)
DAVIE	Scrubbed. Get yer jacket on. Pick up yer cards. On yer way pal! Out the door.
	(ALEC *is playing with yacht, positions fid like bowsprit, bow like mast, tries to make 'sail' with cellophane, can't hold all the separate bits, drops them. DAVIE comes in behind him*)

	Bit of bad news son.
	(*Pause*)
	Ah've lost ma job. They gave me ma books.
ALEC	What'll we dae?
DAVIE	Billy says he might be able tae fix me up wi somethin. Wouldnae be much. (*Shrugs*) Better than nothin. Ach, that was a lousy job anyway. Ah'm better off out ae it. Whatever happens.
	Place is a right mess eh. Amazin how it gets on top of ye.
ALEC	Ah'll shove this in the Glory Hole. Out the road.
	(*Folds up cellophane, puts tools in bag and picks up bow, yacht, carries the lot and exits*)
DAVIE	Ach aye. Not to worry. Never died a winter yet.
	(*Fade lights. Two notes on mouth organ, fade*)

Act two

(*DAVIE is sitting in chair, reading newspaper. ALEC enters, singing.*)

ALEC   (*Sings*)
Give me oil in my lamp keep me burning
Give me oil in my lamp I pray
Halleluja!
Give me oil in my lamp keep me burning
Keep me burning till the break of day

DAVIE   Right wee religious fanatic these days eh? What is it the night then, the bandy hope?

ALEC   Christian Endeavour. Band a Hope's on Thursday.

DAVIE   Ah thought Christian Endeavour was last night?

ALEC   That was just the Juniors. Tonight's the real one.

DAVIE   Are ye no too young?

ALEC   The minister says ah can come.

DAVIE   Is that because ye were top in the bible exam?

ALEC   Top equal. Ah don't know if that's why. He just said ah could come.

DAVIE   Ach well, keeps ye aff the streets!

ALEC   Ah'll be the youngest there.

DAVIE   Mind yer heid in the door. Ye'll get stuck!

ALEC   (*Peering at himself in shaving mirror*) This wee mirror ae yours is really stupid!

DAVIE   What's up wi it?

ALEC   Look at it! There's a big crack doon the middle. The two halfs don't sit right – aw squinty.

DAVIE   Does me fine for shavin.

ALEC   Canny get a good look at yersel. It's dead annoyin.

DAVIE   Ach away ye go!

ALEC   Seen ma bible?

DAVIE   Try lookin where ye left it. (*ALEC looks around*) What's that under thae papers?

ALEC   Where?

DAVIE   There. (*Picks up book*) Naw. It's yer prize fae the Sunday School. (*Reads*) The life of David Livingstone. Good book that. Ah read it when ah was a boy, when ah was in the Boy's Brigade. Funny, it made me want to be a missionary masel. Great White Doctor an that. Off tae darkest Africa.

ALEC   So what happened?

DAVIE	Och, ye know. Just . . . drifted away fae it. Ended up in darkest Govan instead! (*reads label in book*) Glasgow City Mission. First Prize (Equal). Bible knowledge.
ALEC	The questions were a skoosh. Who carried Christ's cross on the way to Calvary? And stuff fae the Catechism. Into what estate did the fall bring mankind? Dead easy. Just a matter of rememberin.
DAVIE	Ach aye, ye take yer brains fae yer mother son. She was clever ye know. Just wurnae the same opportunities when we were young. You stick in son. Get yerself a good education. Get a decent job. Collar and tie. Never have tae take yer jacket off. (*Reads*) First Prize. Ah was in the B.B. for a long time ye know. Sure and Steadfast! (*Sings*)
	Will your anchor hold In the storms of life When the clouds unfold Their wings of strife
ALEC	Ah've still got yer badge for long service.
DAVIE	Ah was a sergeant.
ALEC	Ah've got quite a lot of badges now. There's that Rangers supporter's badge Uncle Billy gave me, wi the lion rampant on it. And the army badge that's shaped like a flame.
DAVIE	Engineers.
ALEC	Christian Endeavour's got a badge. It's a dark blue circle wi a gold rim, and CE in gold letters. Maybe ah'll get one the night. Some ae the teachers have got another badge. It's green wi a gold lamp – a sorta oil lamp, like Aladdin's.
DAVIE	Is there gonnae be any other youngsters there the night?
ALEC	Just Norman. (*Distaste in his voice*)
DAVIE	The Minister's boy. Ye don't like him do ye?
ALEC	He's a big snotter. Thinks he's great.
DAVIE	Was he top in the bible exam as well?
ALEC	Top equal. (DAVIE laughs)
DAVIE	That Minister's a nice wee fella. That time he came up here, after yer mother died, we had quite a wee chat.
ALEC	Aye ye told me.
DAVIE	Ah think he got a surprise. Wi me no goin to church an that, he must've thought ah was a bit ae a heathen. Expected to find me aw bitter, crackin up, y'know?
ALEC	Aye ah know.
DAVIE	But ah wisnae. Ah showed him ma long-service badge fae the B.B. Even quoted scripture at him.
ALEC	Aye.

DAVIE	In my father's house there are many mansions, ah said. That's the text they read at the funeral.
ALEC	Time ah was goin.
DAVIE	He wanted me tae come tae church, but ah cannae be bothered wi aw that. Anyway, you're goin enough for the two ae us these days, eh?
ALEC	Aye. Here's ma bible. (*Picks it up from under newspapers*) Well. Cheerio da.
DAVIE	See ye after son.
	(*ALEC crosses stage, whistling 'Give Me Oil in My Lamp'. Football rolls across. IAN enters*)
IAN	That baw! (*ALEC passes ball to him*) Comin doon for a game?
ALEC	Naw.
IAN	How no?
ALEC	Ah'm goin somewhere.
IAN	The Mission?
ALEC	Aye.
IAN	Again? Ye *never* come oot wi us these days.
ALEC	There's a lot ae things on at the Mission.
IAN	Ye don't have tae go tae them aw!
ALEC	Ah like it.
IAN	Aw well. Suit yersel. (*Dribbles ball round ALEC*)
	(*Chanting*) Will ye come to the mission Will ye come, will ye come Will ye come to the mission Will ye come . . . (*Laughs*)
	Well! (*Calls out as he exits*)
	Gawn yersel!
	Ah'll get ye!
	Ah'll let ye!

ALEC	Ian thought I was soft in the head for going so much to the Mission. He couldn't understand. I felt this glow. It was good to feel good. It had come on stronger since my mother had died.
	    Ah cut across the back courts. Ah could hear Ian and his mates shoutin and laughin in the distance, makin a rammy. Somebody kicked over a midden bin, smashed a bottle. Some auld wifie shouted at them and they scattered. I got ma head down, hurried through a close and out into the street.
	    When ah got to the Mission ah was early. There was only a handful of people, sittin talkin at the front. Nobody even noticed me comin in.

25

Norman was busy stackin hymnbooks. He saw me and went out into the back room. Then the minister waved me over. He introduced me to this middle-aged African couple.

These are our very special guests, he says. Mr and Mrs Lutula. From Africa.

How do you do, we all say, an everybody shakes hands. Then there's this awkward silence. An ah'm standin there like a stookie, no knowin where tae look. Then the conversation sorta picks up again, round about me. But ah can feel the big black woman lookin at me. Tell me, she says – big deep voice like a man's – When did the lord Jesus come into your heart? Pardon? I says. Terrified! She looks right at me. Ah said, when did the Lord Jesus come into your heart, child?

That was what I thought she'd said.
And she wanted an answer. From me!
I looked down at the floor.
I could feel myself blush,
What kind of question was that to ask?
How was I supposed to answer it?
Why didn't she ask me something straightforward?
Who carried Christ's cross on the way to Calvary?
Simon of Cyrene.
Into what estate did the fall bring mankind?
The fall brought mankind into an estate of sin and misery.
(*Tugs at collar*)
It's hot in here. Feelin a wee bit sick.
Ah'll just go outside for a minute, get some fresh air . . .
Ah'm trippin over ma own feet.
Knock over a pile of hymnbooks. Jesus Christ!
Out into the street, walkin faster, runnin, away fae the Mission, through a close, into the back court . . .
The night air was cool. I stopped an leaned against a midden wall. When did the Lord Jesus come into my heart? I could have said it was when my mother died. That would have sounded pious.
But I didn't think it was true. I didn't know. That was it, I didn't know.
If the Lord Jesus had come into my heart, I should know.
The back court was quiet. Just the sound of the TV from this house or that.
Dark tenement blocks.
I kicked over a midden bin, and ran.
Nearer home, I slowed down again.
My father would ask why ah was back so early.

(*Throws down book*)

DAVIE	What's the matter?
ALEC	Nothin
DAVIE	What d'ye mean nothin?
ALEC	Nothin Nothin Nothin!
DAVIE	Yer face is trippin ye. C'mon. Cheer up. It might never happen!

ALEC	Don't annoy me!
DAVIE	Oh ho! Fightin talk! (*Squares up to him, sparring, flicks a few imaginary punches*) C'mon! You an me doon the back wi the jackets aff. Three rounds.
ALEC	(*Sparring, taking him up*) Yes and here we go. Three rounds to decide the flyweight championship of this hoose. Me in the blue corner, the challenger, up-and-coming. The auld man in the red corner . . .
DAVIE	Never mind the auld . . .
ALEC	The auld man . . . the defending champion . . . once beat a man that knew a wumman that maulacated Benny Lynch's granny . . .
DAVIE	(*Drops guard, offended*) Ah knew Benny Lynch! Me an Benny were like that. (*Crosses fingers*)
ALEC	Aye ah know. Ye lent him a fiver ten minutes before he died. (*Swings a punch*)
DAVIE	(*Guard up again*) It was ten bob and it was a week! Terrible state he was in.
ALEC	Probably used the ten bob tae buy his last bottle of plonk. The one that laid him out for the count. (*Pokes DAVIE in stomach*)
DAVIE	Ya wee bugger! (*Rains a flurry of blows, just short of ALEC's face*)
ALEC	(*Giving up*) Awright! Awright! (*DAVIE stops*) You should teach me how tae box. Ah could join a club.
DAVIE	Ach naw son. Boxin's a mug's game. Ye don't want tae waste yer time. Ah didnae stick it. Chucked it when ah met yer mother. Can do yerself serious damage. Ah was lucky. Only got a broken nose.
ALEC	D'ye know that joke? Hey, you wi the broken nose, sing Clementine. Ah havnae got a broken nose an a canny sing. Wallop! (*Holds nose, sings*) Oh ma darlin, Oh ma darlin . . .
DAVIE	(*Laughs*) Definitely a mug's game.
ALEC	Ah was thinkin more just for self-defence an that.
DAVIE	Aye, well. Could show ye the basics ah suppose. Nae harm in knowin how tae look after yerself. Specially in a place like this. Course the likes ae Benny Lynch an these blokes it was the only way tae get out. Fightin. (*Looks at ALEC*) You'll get out usin yer brains but.
ALEC	This exam's comin up.
DAVIE	You'll do it. Make a big difference. Goin tae a good school. Go on tae the University. Decent job.

ALEC   Never have tae take ma jacket off!

(*Puts on jacket, tie, takes pen from inside pocket, sits down at table*)

"By selling a piano for £32 a dealer lost one ninth of the cost price. What would he have gained it he had sold it for £38?"

gained.
£2

Christ that's hard. Ah'll come back to it.

"Two pipes fill a bath in 7½ minutes and 10 minutes respectively, while a third pipe can empty it in 15 minutes. If the three pipes are opened together, in what time will the bath be half full?"

6.7 mins
or 6 mins
40 secs.

Ah'll try the next one.

"A contractor engaged to do a piece of work in 36 days and employed 52 men. After 20 days the work was only half done. How many additional men must he employ to finish the work in the given time?"

God Almighty. Ah cannae do any of these!

Just calm down. Take it easy. There's a knack to it. That's all. Just a matter of seein through it. Take them one at a time. Now.

By selling a piano for £32.

God.

Two pipes fill a bath.

Be nice to have a house wi a bath.

36 days 52 men.

Maybe if ah do wee diagrams. *Picture it.*

Selling a piano.

Do a wee drawin of Fats Domino tinklin the ivories.

Hey, you wid the broken nose, sing Red Sails in the Sunset. Ah ain't got no broken nose an ah can't sing. Wallop!

In what time will the bath be half full?

Did ye ever hear anythin so daft? Who's gonnae run water intae a bath an out again at the same time?

Stupid.
    Just as stupid as me sittin here tryin to work it all out. Bet Ian's out playin football right now. Lucky dog.

52 men 36 days finish the work in the given time.

52 men. One for every week in the year. They're diggin a hole or somethin. Navvies. Takin their jackets off.

36 days hath September. That's no right.

52 men are selling a bath. How long will it take them to play the piano?

(*Holds nose, sings*)

	Red sails in the sunset Way out on the sea . . . Wallop!
	(*Stands up, takes off tie, shoves it in pocket, scrumples up question-paper*)
IAN	(*Entering*) How was the exam?
ALEC	Terrible. Boggin.
IAN	D'ye think ye failed?
ALEC	Aye. English was easy. Arithmetic was murder.
IAN	Ach well. Be a buncha snobs at that school anyway. Aw toffeenosed wee shites.
ALEC	Yer probably right. They havenae even got a fitba team. Play rugby.
IAN	Tellt ye. Snobs.
	(*ALEC kicks scrumpled paper up in the air, takes ball from IAN's feet and kicks it offstage*)
ALEC	Blooter!
	(*IAN chases ball. DAVIE enters with envelope*)
DAVIE	It's the results.
ALEC	You open it.
DAVIE	(*Opens, reads*) You've passed!
ALEC	(*Grabs letter, reads*) "We have pleasure in informing you . . ." Ah've passed! (*Jumps in the air like a footballer*) Wo ho! Ya beauty!
DAVIE	Ah knew ye could do it!
ALEC	Must have got a good mark in the English.
DAVIE	Nae bother.
ALEC	Ah'll go an dae a lap of honour roon the street, eh? (*Punches arms in air*) Ea-sy! Ea-sy!
DAVIE	Yer teacher'll be pleased.
ALEC	(*Reads*) "You have been awarded a bursary . . ." It's great. Means ye get aw yer books an fees an everythin. Ah'll need tae get a school uniform. Blazer an tie an aw that.
DAVIE	That's right. Need tae get ye kitted out.
ALEC	How ye gonnae get the money?
DAVIE	Don't you worry about that. Ah'll think ae somethin.
ALEC	(*Runs, punching the air*) Hullaw! (*IAN enters*) Ah passed ma exam!
IAN	Ah thought ye'd failed?
ALEC	So did ah!
IAN	Aw well, that's it then.
ALEC	Ah couldnae believe it.

IAN	Right wee brainbox, eh! (*Laughs*)
ALEC	What's funny?
IAN	Ah can just see you wi the wee uniform. The wee cap an that!
ALEC	Aye. Well. It's a good school.
IAN	Ye'll need tae build yerself up, for playing rugby!
ALEC	Ye have tae be about 6 feet square an weigh 20 stone.
IAN	There's always cricket! (*Mimics bowler, exaggerated mincing run*) Howzat! (*Laughs*) It's aw boys at that school, intit?
ALEC	Aye.
IAN	Nae lassies?
ALEC	Naw.
IAN	Don't fancy that. Hey, ah'd watch ma bum if ah was you! Suppose ye'll be stayin on, sittin highers an aw that?
ALEC	Hope so.
IAN	Ah couldnae stick it. Imagine still bein at school when yer eighteen or that. Soon as ah'm auld enough ah'm chuckin it. Gettin masel a job.
ALEC	Ye still gonnae try an get in wi yer da?
IAN	Probably. Thing is but, we might be movin away.
ALEC	Where?
IAN	Don't know yet. If ma da gets made redundant he says he'll have tae go where the work is. Could be anywhere. Even England. Corby or that.
ALEC	Too bad.
IAN	Anyway, ah'll be seein ye.
ALEC	Aye. Cheerio.
IAN	An remember, watch yer bum! (*Shouts back as he exits*) Howzat!
	(DAVIE *enters holding blazer,* ALEC *puts it on*)
ALEC	It's a wee bit big.
DAVIE	Ye'll grow intae it. Means ye'll no need a new one next year.
ALEC	How did ye manage tae get it?
DAVIE	Got it on tick. Pay it up. Nae bother. (*Pats* ALEC's *shoulders*) Aw son. Ah wish yer mother could see ye.
ALEC	Ah know.
DAVIE	This is a great chance yer gettin son. Great opportunity. Get yerself a good education. Nothin tae beat it.
ALEC	(*Coming forward*) First conjugation.
Amos, amas, amat, amamus, amatis, amant.

I love, you love, he she or it loves,
We love, you love, they love.

Half the class got belted for not bein able to do that.

Amare.
To love.
Wallop.

Same in music, for the ones that couldn't sightread.
Every Good Boy Deserves Favour.

Or in physics and chemistry if you messed up an experiment.
$C + O_2$ gives CO_2.

Matter can neither be created nor destroyed.

Glasgow made the Clyde, the Clyde made Glasgow.

Amazin the things ye remember.
Algebra Geometry Trigonometry
What *is* the square root of minus one?
Religious Education, one period a week.
The Apostle's Creed.
I believe for every drop of rain that falls, a flower grows.
Elementary calculus.
The approach to Standard English.
Earth hath not anything to show more fair.
Tomorrow and tomorrow and tomorrow.

Future.
Amabo.
I will love.
Electricity. Magnetic flux.

The periodic table of the elements.
Analyse. Parse. Conjugate. Decline.
Prove. Discuss. Explain. With diagrams.
Future Perfect. Nothing to beat it.
A good education.
Tomorrow and tomorrow.
First year, second year, third year bursary.
Fourth year 'O' grade, fifth year Highers.
University here I come.

(*Pause*)

Ready or not. (*Runs off*)

DAVIE   Factory's shuttin doon right enough son. Billy's no so bad, he'll get redundancy money. Ah havnae been there long enough. Still. Not to worry, eh!

ALEC   (*Comes back with record player*) And what does your father do? He's not actually working just now, but he's a sailmaker to trade. Sounds fascinating. Aye.

This has just been lyin in the Glory Hole.

DAVIE   What did ye drag it out for?

ALEC	A boy in ma class lent me some records.
DAVIE	Used tae have a lot of records. Tchaikovsky. John McCormack. Fats Waller.
ALEC	What happened to them?
DAVIE	Had tae sell them. Coupla quid for the lot.
	(ALEC *lifts lid of record player, checks playing arm, dusts it etc . . .*)
	Any idea what ye'd like for yer tea?
ALEC	(*Preoccupied*) Ah'm no bothered.
DAVIE	Maybe yer no bothered, but how about makin a suggestion once in a while!
ALEC	What's the matter?

DAVIE	D'ye think it's easy? Day after day after day, havin tae think ae somethin. An once in a blue moon ah ask for a wee suggestion and what dae ah get?
	(*Mimics boy*) Ah'm no bothered
	               Disnae matter
	               It's aw wan tae me.

ALEC	Aye, but if you're askin me it means *you're* stuck. You cannae think ae anythin an ah'm supposed tae come up wi somethin brilliant. Out the blue. It's no as if we've got a lot of choice. Sausages, mince, fish . . .
DAVIE	How about stew?
ALEC	Well . . .
DAVIE	See, there yar! Ye say yer no bothered but ye don't fancy stew!
ALEC	If ye make stew ah'll eat it. It's just . . .
DAVIE	What?
ALEC	Well, there's more tae stew than just shovin a dod a meat in the pot wi an oxo cube and slappin it on the plate wi a slice a bread.
DAVIE	Oh ah'm helluva sorry. Ah didn't realise we had a gourmet in the family!
ALEC	Ah think ah'll become a vegetarian. Ah was readin this book . . .
DAVIE	Christ is that the next thing?
ALEC	What d'ye mean?
DAVIE	The next craze. We've been through the dinky toys and the fitba an the pop stars. Is it gonnae be long hair an ban the bomb noo?

ALEC	Och forget it! (DAVIE *goes out*)
	    Forget everythin.
	    Wish ye could.
	    There's somethin ah *have* forgotten.
	    Somethin ah've lost.
	    What is it?
	    God knows.

	(*He rushes across, takes record from briefcase and puts it on turntable.*
	Tape '*My Generation*', *The Who.* ALEC *jumps around to the music, jabbing, kicking, aggressive.*
	Music stops dead, lights go dim)
ALEC	What's up? How come there's nae light?
DAVIE	(*Re-entering*) Electricity got cut off son. Couldnae pay the bill.
ALEC	Aw Christ.
DAVIE	It's awright. Ah'll borrow the money. Get it put back on.
ALEC	Ma bursary money'll be comin through this week, can pay it wi that.
DAVIE	Right! That's great!
ALEC	Ah wanted tae buy some things wi it. A shirt an that.
DAVIE	Might still be enough.
ALEC	They charge ye extra for reconnection.
DAVIE	Don't worry. We'll work it out. C'mon! You tell me what kinda shirt ye want an ah'll get it when ah'm in payin the bill. Right?
	(ALEC *nods*)
	Nae bother. Hey there's a coupla pies in the oven. Candlelight dinner for two sir?
	(ALEC *smiles in spite of himself. They exit*)
	(BILLY *enters, wearing overalls carrying painpots, brushes etc. small canvas bag over shoulder containing sandwiches, flask of tea etc. He is cleaning paint from his hands*)
BILLY	(*Calling off*) Hey Michaelangelo! Ye finished that ceiling?
IAN	(*Off*) Aye.
BILLY	Ah'm oot here when yer ready.
IAN	(*Entering, also in overalls, cleaning hands*) What's for wur piece?
BILLY	Don't know. Cheese or spam or somethin.
IAN	(*Looks in bag, opens sandwich*) Cheese. (*Opens second sandwich*) Spam.
BILLY	Ah'm easy. (IAN *passes him sandwich. They eat*) Piece perfect piece!
IAN	Piecework! (*They laugh*) Feels funny workin on a Saturday.
BILLY	Aye. Ah'm sorry yer missin the match. But just think ae the money yer rakin in wi aw this overtime. Two nights an a Saturday an Sunday.
IAN	(*Noncommittal*) Aye.
BILLY	An it's no as if it's gonnae be every week. They're just in a hurry tae get this place open on time.
IAN	What kinda shop's it gonnae be?
BILLY	Licensed Grocer's ah think.

	Be nice that, havin yer ain business. Ye know, just after the war, when ah got ma demob money, ah was gonnae go in wi yer Uncle Davie.
IAN	Daein what?
BILLY	He had this idea tae raise poultry! He'd read a coupla books. Eggs were still on ration ye see. He reckoned we'd make a fortune. Fresh farm eggs!
IAN	So how d'ye no dae it?
BILLY	Och. Ah thought it was takin too much ae a chance.
IAN	Ah like Uncle Davie.
BILLY	Aw aye. His heid's in the clouds mind ye!
IAN	Ah got a letter fae Alec. He's still at school. Can ye imagine!
BILLY	Be worth it when he's finished. Ach aye. Be awright bein yer ain boss right enough. Naebody tellin ye what tae dae. A wee paint shop would dae fine eh? Need tae make sure it was gonnae work but. Line up a coupla nice wee contracts. Like paintin the Forth Bridge!
IAN	That goes on forever.
BILLY	That's right. Just get tae the end an it's time tae start aw over again.
IAN	Imagine bein stuck up there on wan a thae big girders. The wind blowin aboot ye!
BILLY	Bad enough when ah worked in the yards. Daein a boat in the dry dock. Slung over the side in wan a thae wee cradles. Fifty feet aff the grun! Thing is tae, ah've never had much ae a head for heights.
IAN	How did ye manage?
BILLY	Just had tae. Nothin else for it. Keep yer eyes on the wee bit yer workin on an don't look doon!
IAN	Makes yer hands go aw sweaty just thinkin about it!
BILLY	Ach, ye get used tae it. Same as anythin else. We'll have ye up there spraypaintin a big gas tank. Or wan a thae oilrigs.
IAN	Ah could spray ma name on it. Ian Rules! OK!
BILLY	Catch ye at that lark an ye'll get a thick ear.
IAN	Och da!
BILLY	Just tellin ye.
IAN	See when you were in the army, did ye like it?
BILLY	It was awright. Ah was lucky mind ye. Didnae see a lot of action. No like some poor buggers. How, ye thinkin about joinin up?
IAN	Ah was readin an advert in the paper. (*Stands with imaginary machinegun*) Join the Professionals.

BILLY	Shows ye a guy playing fitba? Jumpin aff a tank? Sunbathin?
IAN	Aye.
BILLY	They don't show ye the hauf ae it. You'd likely get sent tae Belfast.
IAN	Fight the I.R.A. Be like the Battle ae the Boyne aw over again!
BILLY	It's no just playin at cowboys ye know. These bastards arenae kiddin. Sunbathin by Christ!
IAN	The Navy might be better. See a bit ae the world.
BILLY	See the sea! Don't get me wrong. Ah've got nothin against it. Queen an Country an aw that. It's just that . . .
IAN	Ah've never even been tae London.
BILLY	Yer no missin much!
IAN	But you can only say that cause ye've been.
BILLY	Look, aw ah'm sayin is don't rush intae anythin, awright? Wance ye sign up that's it. For three year or five year or whatever. Canny say ye don't like it an come runnin hame!
IAN	Ah know that! Anyway ah never *said* ah was gonnae join up. Just said ah was *thinkin* about it.

BILLY	Aye.
	   We should be thinkin about finishin this job, eh?
	   Ye fit?

IAN	Aye.

(*They gather up their things*)

BILLY	Green an gold he wants. (*Shakes head*) What can ye dae!

(*They exit*)

(*Enter ALEC. He sits at table, reading*)

DAVIE	(*Off, singing*)
	   Where the blue of the night
	   Meets the gold of the day
	   Someone waits for me.

(*DAVIE enters, drunk*)

DAVIE	Hey, yer auld da knocked it off at the bookies. Nae bother! Went in for a wee half tae celebrate. Then ah met Kenny. Don't know if ye remember him – bloke ah used tae work wi in the yards.
	   Anyway, that was it. Coupla rounds, wee blether – ye know how it is.
	   Christ is that the time?
	   Not to worry. Last orders please. Time gents!
	   Never mind.
	   Was a good night. Good Company. Know what ah mean?
	   Nae harm in it. Coupla halfs. Nice.

(*Noticing ALEC*) Yawright son?

ALEC	(Not looking up) Aye.
DAVIE	Ach aye. Yirra good boy. What ye readin?
ALEC	A book.
DAVIE	Naw! *Whit* book!
ALEC	David Copperfield. Got an exam next week.
DAVIE	Dickens, eh? Now yer talkin. Ah've read aw his books. The lot. Got them all out the library. Used tae read a lot ye know. Dickens is the greatest. David Copperfield is it?
ALEC	That's what ah said.
DAVIE	Mr Micawber. Somethin'll turn up, eh? 　Income twenty pounds, expenditure nineteen pounds nineteen and six: result happiness. 　Income twenty pounds, expenditure twenty pounds and sixpence: result . . . (Shrugs) Not to worry. Hey, ah got ye crisps. Bottle ae iron brew. (Puts them on table)
ALEC	(Grudging) Thanks.
DAVIE	Any chance ae a cuppa tea?
ALEC	There's some left in the pot. (DAVIE pours dregs)
DAVIE	(Sings) 　Where the blue of the night 　Meets the gold of the day (To ALEC) Cheer up. (No response) C'mon. (Spars)
ALEC	Chuck it will ye!
DAVIE	Torn face.
ALEC	Ah didnae know where ye wur.
DAVIE	Och . . .
ALEC	Might have been under a bus or anythin.
DAVIE	(Sighs) Look. Ah'm sorry, awright? Just . . . wan a these things, ye know.
ALEC	Aye ah know.
DAVIE	Good company. Nae harm in it. Didnae even have a lot tae drink. It's just good tae relax. 　Wee refreshment. Ach aye. The patter was good tae. 　Kenny's a great Burns man. Could recite Tam O'Shanter tae ye just like that! Yer sittin talkin away and he'll come out wi a line fae it. 　Fast by an ingle, bleezing finely 　Wi reamin swats that drank divinely 　Great stuff eh? Poetry! 　Reamin swats! Anythin for eatin?

ALEC	Naw.
DAVIE	Nothin?
ALEC	Not a thing.
DAVIE	What about that tin a soup?
ALEC	Ah had it for ma tea.
DAVIE	Oh aye. An the creamed rice?
ALEC	Ah ate that tae.
DAVIE	Themorra ah'll get a nice bit steak. Have it wi chips. Fried tomatoes! Is there no even any bread?
ALEC	Nothin.
DAVIE	Can ah take a couple ae yer crisps?
ALEC	Help yerself.
DAVIE	Just a couple. (*Eats crisps, swigs iron brew from bottle*) Reamin swats! There was this lassie there. In the company like. Peggy her name was. Friend ae Kenny's. Helluva nice tae talk tae. Know what ah mean? Just a really nice person.
ALEC	Oh aye. (*Bangs down book*)
DAVIE	What's up wi you?
ALEC	Oh nothin. Nothin at all. Everythin's just hunky-dory!
	(*Wipes bottle, swigs. Looks suspiciously at* DAVIE)
	Did you gamble wi that bursary money?
DAVIE	Just a coupla quid. There was gonnae be nothing left after ah'd paid the light bill. Had tae take a chance.
ALEC	Did ye *pay* the bill?
DAVIE	First thing themorra mornin.
ALEC	Don't suppose ye got ma shirt either?
DAVIE	Themorra. Ye can wear it at the weekend. Look like a real spiv! Ah hear ye've got a wee girlfriend!
ALEC	Who told you that?
DAVIE	Oh, a wee bird told me! What's the lassie's name?
ALEC	What does it matter?
DAVIE	Can you no talk tae me these days? Can ye no tell me *anythin*? Think ah came fae another planet.
ALEC	One time when ah was really wee ah went tae this birthday party – wee lassie doon the road. Must have been ma first party, and we played aw the wee kissin games, ye know. Postman's knock. Bee Baw Babbity. Anyway, ah came hame dead excited. An you said, how was the party?

	An ye said, did ye kiss the girls and make them cry? An ah was that embarrased, ah walloped ye wan. Slapped ye right in the face. An then ye got mad at me.
DAVIE	Ah'm no suprised!
ALEC	But ye didnae skelp me or anythin. Ye just shoved me away and told me ah was a bad bad bad boy.
DAVIE	Ah don't even remember it.
ALEC	Bad. Bad. Bad. Made me feel dirty. Been better if ye'd just hit me back. But ye didnae. Ye held a grudge.
DAVIE	Christsake, you're the wan that remembers it. You're the wan that's holdin the grudge. Ah mean it was nothin!
ALEC	Aye, tae you! That's what ah mean!
DAVIE	Ah give up!
ALEC	Ye always do.
DAVIE	Now that's no nice. That's a bit below the belt.
ALEC	Look at the state ae us. We're livin like bloody Steptoe an Son! Nae light. Place is like a midden. When did we last gie it a good clean? Needs gutted. Look at it!
DAVIE	It's hard son. it's no easy on yer own.
ALEC	So ye go an get bevvied. Forget it all.
DAVIE	Ye'd think ah came in steamin every night! Christ ah need a wee break once in a while. Like the night. Nae harm in it. Good company. Wee sing song. Right gents, a wee bit order there. One singer one song. That lassie Peggy's a rare singer. Sang Honky Tonk Angels. She's the one ah told ye about.
ALEC	(*Sarcastic*) The really nice person.
DAVIE	She wis.
ALEC	Who was that lady I saw you with last night? That was no lady, that was a really nice person.
DAVIE	Nae harm in it.
ALEC	It's always the same. Every time ye meet a wumman she's a really really really nice person. Why don't ye just admit that ye fancy her?

(DAVIE *slaps him, exits*)

Ach aye, yirra good boy son. Wallop!
    Bad. Bad. Bad.

(*Pause*)

Wallop.

(*Darkness. Spotlight on ALEC*)

I keep goin back.
>What is it I'm tryin to remember?
>What is it I'm tryin to say?
>There's somethin I've lost. Something I've forgotten.
>Sometimes in the middle of the night . . .
>What is it I'm looking for?
>God knows.

(*Lights up. He crosses over, picks up yacht. DAVIE is sitting in chair, staring into empty hearth*)

Remember this?

DAVIE	Eh? (*Looks*) Oh aye. It's freezin.
ALEC	Nae coal left?
DAVIE	Ah'll get some themorra, when the dole money comes.
ALEC	Ye wouldnae believe some of the stuff that's in the Glory Hole.
DAVIE	Is that where ye wur? Terrible draught comin in that door.
ALEC	Hey, d'ye remember that poem ye used to tell me?
DAVIE	Poem?
ALEC	About the yacht. (*Recites*) Ah had a yacht Y'ought tae see it I actually thought you wrote it, ye know – made it up yourself.
DAVIE	Och naw. Ah learned it fae ma father. Ah wis just passing it on.
ALEC	Ah had a yacht . . . (*Shivers*) Hey it really is cold. There must be some auld stuff in that Glory Hole we could burn.
DAVIE	That's a great idea.
ALEC	Place needs gutted anyway. Might as well make a start. (*Goes out*)

(*DAVIE scrumples up papers for fire, rolls some up into 'doughnut' shapes. ALEC returns with box of stuff*)

Coupla auld books for a start. (*Reads*) The Approach to Standard English. (*Throws it over*) Ma auld hymnbook (*flicks through pages*).

DAVIE	Cannae burn a hymnbook.
ALEC	How no?
DAVIE	It's just no right.
ALEC	(*Throws hymnbook to DAVIE*) Hey! (*Reads from catechism*) Into what estate did the Fall bring mankind?
DAVIE	What?
ALEC	Catechism. What is man's chief end?
DAVIE	(*Parrot-fashion*) Man's chief end is to glorify God and to enjoy Him forever.

Ah'd forgotten all that! Used to know it all. Amazin how ye forget.

ALEC	But part of ye remembers everythin. What's the furthest back you can remember?
DAVIE	Don't know. Never really thought about it. Ah remember goin tae school. Must have been five.
ALEC	Ah remember bein a baby, in the pram. Honest tae God. Ah remember bein aw tucked up, and the pram shooglin along, and the rain patterin on the hood. Nobody ever believes me.
DAVIE	Ah believe ye.
ALEC	Ah was readin that ye can remember right back before ye were born. Right back tae the womb.
DAVIE	Never heard ae that!
ALEC	In fact some folk say ye remember it aw the time, away at the back ae yer mind. Like part ae ye never really forgets, an ye've always got a sorta yearnin tae get back tae it.
DAVIE	(Remembering answer to question) The fall brought mankind into an estate of sin and misery!
ALEC	We got some stuff about other religions in school. Hinduism an Buddhism an that. Ye know, some ae them talk about God bein male and female. Father an Mother. An some ae them don't talk about God at all.
DAVIE	(Uncomfortable) Ye have tae believe in somethin. Otherwise . . . (Shrugs)
ALEC	In one ae the Buddhist books ah read there was a story about a monk that burned a wooden statue ae the Buddha. 'What d'ye dae that for?' they asked him. "It's freezin" he says. (Laughs) Ah think the idea was that everythin's holy. Or nothin. (Chucks catechism across) There ye go! (DAVIE puts it to one side, along with hymnbook. ALEC takes sea-shell from box, holds it up, puts it to his ear) You can still hear the sea! Ah used to think it was the actual sea ye could hear. Whatever sea the shell came from. As if the shell had a memory of the sea right inside it. Naw. No a memory, that's the wrong word. More like an echo. As if it had been caught inside. (Hands shell to DAVIE, who self-consciously holds it to his ear, sighs, puts shell down) Remember this? (Holds up torch)
DAVIE	Aye. (ALEC breathes on torch, polishes it on his sleeve, clicks button)
ALEC	Disnae work.
DAVIE	Batteries'll be dead.
ALEC	Pity. Could've used it tae see intae that recess. Hey, look, it's still got a dent in it where ye thumped that guy.

DAVIE	What a job that wis. Terrible. Ah'm better on the broo than daein that, any day. That bookie's done awright for himself. Two shops he's got. Nae back closes for him noo.
ALEC	Mainsail. That was yer name.
DAVIE	That's right. Ye remember!
ALEC	Tryin the pools!
DAVIE	Still tryin. Ye never know.
ALEC	(*Opens torch, shakes it, peers inside*) Batteries are stuck. Aw covered in green mouldy stuff. What makes it go like that?
DAVIE	Don't know. Just time. Just . . . time. What else is there?
ALEC	(*Looking in box again*) Coupla old comics. Superman. Blackhawk. Creepy Worlds. (*Reads*) Mysterious Voyage. Journey into the Unknown. (*Throws them over*) Another coupla books. Now these are *really* auld. Peoples of the World, and How the Other Man Lives.
DAVIE	Think we picked them up at a jumble sale.
ALEC	Listen to this! The British Working Man. (*Reads*) The life of the British industrial worker differs only in detail from that of his world counterpart. His housing conditions were once poor, but have been greatly improved.
DAVIE	(*Looking at him*) Have they?
ALEC	(*Continues*) The variety of British industrial occupations is almost endless. The worker may be a skilled man or a labourer. He is perhaps at his best in skilled individual occupations as, for example, in the many aspects of shipbuilding or engineering. He works without rush, but consistently.
DAVIE	Aw!
ALEC	(*Continues*) Our man has probably his special interests: football is most certainly one of them. He will follow the fortunes of his local team with great enthusiam – probably in his youth he was an active player himself. His summer interest in cricket will not be so emotional, but is often deep.
DAVIE	Cricket?
ALEC	(*Continues*) By American standards the British worker is not highly paid, but then the cost of living is much lower.
DAVIE	Nice tae know.
ALEC	(*Continues*) He is greatly interested in social questions. Better housing, old age pensions, security of employment – on these he is now seeing practical results. Education, too, is an increasingly important subject, and many men seek for their sons better opportunities than they themselves enjoyed in their youth. (*Turns pages*) Goes on like this for about ten pages. Then it goes on to Tribes of Africa, and The American Way of Life.

DAVIE	Great stuff.
ALEC	(*Passes over book*) See what the other one's about. How the Other Man Lives. (*Reads*) The Other Man's job so frequently appears more attractive than one's own.
DAVIE	Specially if ye havnae got wan! Don't suppose there's anythin about sailmakers? Or redundant tick-men!
ALEC	(*Reads*) Farmer . . . Coalminer . . . Ah don't believe it! Bookmaker! (*Turns pages, reads*) Here, this is good . . . In theory an astute bookmaker should be able to make his book so that he cannot lose. This, however is accomplished only if he can induce a sufficient number of punters to back little-fancied and long-priced animals.
DAVIE	Mugs! Like me!
ALEC	(*Continues*) If there is money for only two or three horses, then the cleverest bookmaker cannot level his book.
DAVIE	Makes yer heart bleed for them, doesn't it!
	(*ALEC shuts book, throws it over to DAVIE*)
DAVIE	Ach aye!
ALEC	What is it that gets intae ye? Wi the bettin ah mean?
DAVIE	Ah don't know. Just wan a these things. Ah suppose it's the feelin you've at least got a *chance*. Is there any wood in there? The paper just flares up then dies.
	(*ALEC empties out contents of box, hands box to DAVIE*)

DAVIE	Great. (*Starts breaking up box, ALEC goes out, comes back with canvas tool-bag, cane bow. Fires imaginary arrow*) Bring me my bow of burning gold, eh?
	    (*ALEC breaks bow for fire*)
	    That's more like it. (*Warms himself*)
	    That's the stuff.

ALEC	(*Taking tools from canvas bag*) Look at this.
DAVIE	God. Ma auld sailmakin tools. (*Takes wooden marlinspike*) Ah was an apprentice when ah was your age. Hard work it wis tae. Ah worked on the Queen Mary ye know.
ALEC	Aye.
DAVIE	Worked on destroyers durin the War. Made gun-covers, awnings, tarpaulins. Made this wee bag!
ALEC	Did ye?
DAVIE	Oh aye. Used tae make leather wallets an things. Made a shopping bag for yer mother. Made you a swing! Wi a big sorta bucket seat. Used tae hang it in the doorway there.
ALEC	Ah remember! You could still be makin things. Sellin them.

(DAVIE *nods, shrugs*)

Could ye no go back tae yer trade?

DAVIE   Nae demand. Was different durin the War. They needed us then awright. Reserved occupation it was. Meant ah couldnae sign up. Been goin downhill since then but. Yards shuttin doon. Look at Harland's. Or where it was. Just a big empty space covered wi weeds.
     Yer Uncle Billy had the right idea. Took his redundancy money an moved tae Aberdeen. Doin all right.

ALEC   Ian's an Aberdeen supporter now.

DAVIE   Billy'll disown him for that!

ALEC   Did you ever think about movin?

DAVIE   Thought about it. (*Shrugs*) Thing is Billy bein a painter had more chance ae a job. Ah backed a loser right fae the start. Then it got even worse. They started bringin in aw the manmade fibres, usin machines. Got lassies daein hauf the work. Dead loss.
     So for God's sake you dae somethin wi your life!
     At least we'll be gettin out ae this place when they pull it doon. Get rehoused. Fresh start.

ALEC   Ah've been thinkin da. When ah go tae the University ah might get a wee place ae ma own. Wee bedsit or somethin. Over near the Uni.

DAVIE   Oh aye. Will that no be dear?

ALEC   Shouldnae be too bad.

DAVIE   Whatever ye think.

ALEC   Ah'll see what happens.

DAVIE   Aye.

(*Silence between them. DAVIE takes up tools*)

These are made fae lignum vitae.

ALEC   That's Latin. Wood of life.

DAVIE   Hardest wood in the world. Should burn nice an slow. (*Puts in fire*) Thae other tools can go in the midden sometime. (*Watches fire*) Is there anythin else?

ALEC   There's this. (*Indicates chair*)

DAVIE   This is part of the furniture we got when we were married. Got it in Galpern's. That's him that was the Lord Provost. Solid stuff it is too.
     Nobody takes the care any more.
     Nobody's interested in this auld stuff.
     (*He is talking himself into being sad*)
     Ah remember when we bought it.
     Seems a shame tae break it up. Still
     It's a shame tae freeze as well, isn't it.

(*Breaks up chair, they watch it burn*)

ALEC	(*Picks up yacht*) That just leaves this.
DAVIE	Yer Uncle Billy painted it.
ALEC	You were always gonnae fix it up for me. Ah could always imagine it. Like that song. Red sails in the sunset.
DAVIE	Ah always meant to. Just . . .
ALEC	Just never did.
DAVIE	Story a ma life.

ALEC	(*Comes forward with yacht*) When the last bit of furniture had burned down, I wedged the yacht in the grate.
	   The flames licked round it.
	   The paint began to blister and bubble.
	   Then the wood of the hull caught and burned.
	   And the yacht had a sail of flame.
	   And it sailed in the fire, like a Viking longboat, out to sea in a blaze with the body of a dead chief.
	   And the wood burned to embers. And the iron keel clattered onto the hearth. (*Drops yacht*)
	   May God bless her and all who sail in her!
	   Star of the Sea. Stella Maris.
	   Amabo. I will love.
	   Amazin the things ye remember.
	   Glasgow made the Clyde, the Clyde made Glasgow.
	   Matter can neither be created nor destroyed.
	   Ah had a yacht
	   Y'ought tae see it.

DAVIE	Put it in the canal. Ye can all see it.

(*Fade lights*)

(*Tape: Fats Domino, Red Sails in the Sunset*)